"God's Spirit is ca
prayer. Methods ar
Lord is seeking a pe
and walk in intimacy with him. Drew Meyer himself lives this
call and has articulated it wonderfully well. *Discovering the
Power of Prayer* is both practical and profound. It is a gift to all
who would hear."

DR. JAMES BRADFORD,
author of *Lead So Others Can Follow* and
Pastor of Central Assembly Springfield, Missouri

"Too often prayer is viewed as an impersonal source of power
or a formula to get what we want from God. Pastor Drew
Meyer powerfully captures the true biblical essence of prayer
in this book, *Discovering the Power of Prayer*. A personal relationship with God is at the core of what prayer is really all
about. The book announces that premise at the very onset of
the study: "Prayer is an experience and expression of a love
relationship initiated by the grace of God." The truths Pastor
Drew so clearly articulates here have the potential to revolu-
tionize your prayer life and your relationship to God! Read it,
implement the principles and I am convinced you will experience a spiritual empowerment that will move your prayer
life from a dry discipline to an overwhelming delight."

GARY PILCHER,
Pastor of Berean Assembly of God, Altoona, Iowa,
former pastor of LifePointe Church, and Iowa Assistant
Superintendent of the Assemblies of God

"In the years that I have known Drew he has demonstrated that he is a man of prayer. He understands the power of prayer and the importance of teaching others about prayer. His passion for seeking God through prayer is clearly seen in *Discovering the Power of Prayer*. Many people are not sure how they are to pray. This book gives a clear explanation of how to seek God in prayer. You will be blessed by *Discovering the Power of Prayer* and if you apply the key points Drew teaches regarding prayer, your faith in God will grow and your prayers will become more effective."

DR. RANDY ROBERTSON,
former pastor of LifePointe Church

"When Drew enrolled at NDSU he was one of only three students that I fast tracked to leadership as a freshman. He was also a part of a group of young men who came early in the morning to our church and prayed earnestly for our Chi Alpha ministry. That prayer meeting took our ministry to a whole new level of fruitfulness. I have been an observer as Drew has patiently but fervently prayed his way through the major decisions of life the last ten years. Serving as Senior Pastor of LifePointe Church Drew is well qualified by God and his experiences to write this book on prayer. I encourage everyone reading these pages to feast on the scripturally based pray truths they contain. Prepare to grow in your prayer life and relationship with Jesus Christ as you read and study this wonderful book."

BRAD LEWIS,
North Dakota District Chi Alpha Director

"As a spiritual leader, one of the most important tasks before you is creating a culture where prayer thrives. It has been said that prayerlessness is the ultimate pride. I honor you for resourcing your faith community in prayer for, after all, prayer does not make A difference. It makes THE difference. I stand with you and believe for the restoration of families, for dry and weary souls to bloom, and for your city to feel and sense the impact of prayer rising before the face of God."

HEATH ADAMSON,
author of *The Bush Always Burns* and
Chief of Staff for Convoy of Hope

"Pastor Drew will teach you prayer is the most powerful tool we have as followers of Jesus. I've learned there are no magic formulas, nor any step-by-step plans guaranteeing the results we seek. I've seen prayers answered instantly, a man raised from the dead, physical healings, and provision. Yet, at other times, answers are delayed. I was instantly healed of an incurable disease, Multiple Sclerosis. My healing was the result of hundreds of prayers, by many people, over an extended period of time. The prayers were answered at the right moment, where God's Word, faith, and God's timing intersected. You will not be disappointed as you learn to make prayer an important priority in your life. Be blessed in this journey!"

BOB HENKLEMAN,
District Presbyter of the Iowa Assemblies of God

"This book is a practical tool that reminds us to enjoy the companionship and power of Jesus Christ through prayer."

RICHARD LANG,
World Missionary and U.S.A. Missionary,
Church Planter & Church Developer

12 TRUTHS THAT CAN AWAKEN THE
CHURCH TO PRAY

DISCOVERING THE
POWER
OF
PRAYER

WRITTEN BY

DREW MEYER

Printed by CreateSpace, An Amazon.com Company
Drew Meyer Press
409 13th St
Ames, IA 50010
www.livethemessage.org

Unless otherwise specified, Scripture quotations used in this book are taken from the 2016 edition of the Holy Bible, English Standard Version®. ESV®. Copyright © by Crossways Bibles, Wheaton, IL.

Scripture quotations marked NLT are from the NLT® Bible (Holy Bible, New Living Translation®. Copyright © by Tyndale House Publishers, Carol Stream, IL.

Book Layout © 2017 BookDesignTemplates.com
Cover Design: Drew Meyer
Cover Photo: Shutterstock

Discovering the Power of Prayer / Drew Meyer. -- 1st ed.
ISBN 978-1790128990

This book is dedicated to the faithful and faith-filled followers of Jesus at LifePointe Church in Ames, IA. It is such an honor to pursue Jesus alongside this church family.

"The only power that God yields to is prayer."
—LEONARD RAVENHILL
Why Revival Tarries

Contents

• • •

Foreword

A group of climbers set out to scale a mountain peak. They prepared for weeks in advance and there was tremendous excitement when the morning of the climb arrived. About half-way up the ascent, the group stopped at a chalet. The warmth and comfort of the beautiful facility was very attractive to the weary climbers, and several decided to remain inside as the others continued their ascent. Those who remained inside had an interesting conversation about climbing. They enjoyed a full buffet and relaxed with hot chocolate as they retired to the large picture window that looked out toward the mountain's summit. As they viewed the other climbers struggling up the mountain, the room grew quiet. Those who rested realized what they were missing. They were not struggling, but they were not experiencing the adventure. They weren't tired or cold, but they couldn't see the view from the mountain's peak. They would have a story to tell, but they would not have THE story to tell.

Adventures are challenging, but they produce rewards that the non-adventurous never experience. The wonderful (and sometimes frightening) thing about an adventure is that you can't know exactly what is coming next. You often face challenges you didn't expect. Typically, adventurers learn something. Each new experience provides an opportunity to discover something about the world around you... Or to learn something about yourself.

Taking an adventure with a group of people produces extra rewards because you have shared stories to tell. You know your fellow adventurers better than you did before, and discover people you can depend upon. Together, you learn how your shared capacities are greater than the sum of your individual strengths and abilities.

I have been on an adventure over the past 46 years. This adventure hasn't included mountain climbing, or deep-sea diving (I actually get seasick trying to snorkel!). Mine has been a prayer adventure. I've joined my faith with hundreds of different believers in prayer. We have literally seen bodies healed and spirits changed. Mothers who were told they would never conceive have given birth to healthy babies. We have experienced financial miracles.

My adventuring friends and I have also faced challenges together. At times, it seemed like our prayers were unanswered. In the midst of it all, however, we were discovering more about ourselves and more about our relationship with God and His kingdom. That's the way adventures work.

You and your church are embarking on a prayer adventure. Pastor Drew Meyer is your able climbing companion and guide. He has experienced the challenges and the breath-taking views that are part of the adventure. This book contains a series of trail markers. It's not a detailed map. It is designed to keep you on course, but leaves room for your personal adventure.

You have the added benefit of taking this adventure with others in your church. My prayer is that you will choose to leave the comfort of what you have experienced so far, and that you will experience the adventure together. I pray that your personal times of prayer will be filled with a sense of God's presence. I pray that your times of prayer, worship and the study of God's Word together will be energized with passion and the life-changing power of God.

Jump in. Don't hold back. Commit to take this adventure together. You'll see some amazing and unexpected things. And your life will never be the same.

Tom Jacobs
Iowa District Superintendent
of the Assemblies of God

Introduction

I counsel you to buy from me gold refined by fire...
Revelation 3:18a

Why a book on prayer? Haven't many others written on prayer already? Is prayer so complicated that yet another book or explanation is needed?

Lately, I've felt that our church is sitting on the edge of something great, a greatness defined by true, lasting impact on our families, neighborhoods and cities. But what if those great things in God would only come to pass if we took part in the age-old kingdom practice of prayer? And likewise, what if we missed out on what God had for us because we didn't have the urgency in our hearts to pray?

In Revelation 3:18 Jesus says, "I counsel you to buy from me gold refined by fire, so that you may be rich, and white garments so that you may clothe yourself and the shame of your nakedness may not be seen, and salve to anoint your eyes, so that you may see." Jesus is telling the church in Laodicea that they have the riches of heaven available to them, but their contentment and apathy blind them to what is right in front of them.

You can think of this book as a pastor's letter of personal discipleship. One of my deepest desires as a pastor is to see people walk in daily relationship with God. I want every person to hear what Jesus is saying and buy this "gold refined in the fire." Plain and simple, I desire to see as many people as possible experience the life-giving reality of walking with God. And the key to this is people experiencing real prayer. But I have found that to be a difficult task. We can talk about prayer. We can say we value prayer. But those things don't give people the experience of prayer.

There are many resources available for prayer—including books that have impacted my prayer life, podcasts/sermons, or apps—they all provide valuable insight into prayer. But for our church they are not personal. With that said, let me give you some background on my journey with prayer.

When I was 20 years old, I remember being on a weekend Chi Alpha retreat. Towards the end of this retreat, one of the leaders of the weekend said something that I just couldn't shake. He said, "I challenge you to really seek God with your life. I believe that if you devote one hour a day to prayer for 30 days straight, your life will never be the same." I'm sure I had heard a similar challenge at different times in my life. But for some reason, this time it resonated with me in a unique way.

I did not have ministry aspirations at that point in my life. I was simply intrigued by the potential power of prayer that I had yet to experience. Over the days that followed, a small group of college students began meeting at a local church before our morning classes. We began seeking God. We began to learn to truly experience prayer. Many of us were set on fire with genuine relationship with God for the first time. Needless to say, that small prayer gathering, which was supposed to last 30 days, lasted beyond the 30 days. And something really did begin to change in my life. God worked in the hearts of some simple college students, and that work translated into our daily lives. Soon God began to do miraculous things, and we began to see an amazing move of God where many people came to know Him.

I believe that something similar will take place in our church. God wants to use us for great change in the world around us, and I believe that change will happen through prayer. This book is not intended to be a final authority on, or even a new insight into, prayer. It's not meant to replace any prior works on prayer. I decided to write this book on prayer because I am convinced of the power of prayer. I am convinced that humbly calling on the name of Jesus changes situations and trajectories. I decided that writing a book specifically for our church with the intent of sparking a fresh faith in prayer would be worth the time and effort.

Writing on prayer is an interesting endeavor because prayer in its most effective state is simple, raw and purely relational. Prayer is not a contrived formula of just-the-right words. Nor is it an intense mental exercise only attained through years of practice. Prayer is an experience and expression of a love relationship initiated by the grace of God. So, this is not a book of methods. This is a book that lays out truths on prayer with the intent of drawing more people into a lifestyle of prayer that changes the world.

Prayer is an experience and expression of a love relationship initiated by the grace of God.

Prayer has to be experienced. Prayer cannot be overly strategized. Prayer is responsive and therefore I have found that the best way to experience the life-changing power of prayer is to immediately respond to the God that reveals truth to you. That is why I encourage you throughout this book to take time to respond to God. Allow truth revealed to push you towards truth experienced. Many times, our prayers of response are simply acknowledging to God our wrong thinking and professing the truth of His Word in our lives.

Experience It

Each chapter of this book focuses on one truth from Scripture about prayer, and is meant to be consumable in one sitting. Each chapter ends with a space for response titled "Experience It." It's my desire that you take the time to reflect on how you can actively respond to each truth laid out in this book. Part of the response is "Confession", which simply means a confession of wrong thinking, doubts or lies you have believed about God or your relationship with Him. The next part is "Profession", which means profession of the truth in your own words. I pray this book truly awakens our church to pray like never before.

CHAPTER 1

Seek the Face of God

Truth #1
God created us for relationship with Him.

You have said, 'Seek My face.'
My heart says to You, 'Your face, Lord, do I seek.
Psalm 27:8

First and foremost, prayer is relational. It must be seen in that light. I believe prayer is stripped of much of its power if it's not seen as simple conversation and relationship with God. Prayer is not a good luck charm based on the right combination of words. Prayer is not about fulfilling some obligation to God. Prayer is also not just about our needs. The power of prayer lies within something so much more.

I got engaged to the love of my life towards the end of college. And I believed I had a good strategy. I thought I would propose to her in the late spring, and spend the summer drilling water wells in central Africa as she planned the wedding. I thought I would simply return for another semester of engineering school and a wedding. I didn't have a clue when it came to wedding planning, so I thought I should just leave that up to her. Fortunately, she did say "Yes" when I popped the question and it did work out for me to go to Africa for the summer. What I didn't take into consideration is how much I would miss the face-to-face conversation with my future bride while I was away.

Getting engaged was a fresh new chapter in our love story that sparked a new depth of relationship I hadn't previously experienced. I soon began to realize that my heart ached to see the love of my life. About once a week we were able to talk on the phone. We wrote emails back and forth, but nothing compared to the face-to-face conversation between two people who have a real relationship of love and friendship. Face-to-face conversation naturally includes the ebb and flow of dialog and can even include pauses in the conversation.

In Psalm 27, David references the voice of God in his life saying, "Seek My face." David recognized that God was telling him to seek Him, meaning to let God be his sole desire. But God told him more than just to seek Him. He said, "Seek My face." But didn't God earlier say to Moses that no one would see God? Why should we be seeking His face?

David captured something that is central to prayer. Prayer is conversation. At its best, prayer is stripped of the adornments of show and facades. As David made himself available to hear from God, he began to understand that God created him for relationship with Him. God's call to seek His face was a call back to what He created David for, relationship with God. Before sin (Genesis 3), Adam and Eve had unimpeded communion with God. God walked with Adam in the cool of the morning.

Relationship with God is not a fringe benefit of the gospel (the good news of God's redemption through Jesus). Relationship is what God restored through His Son. What God set in motion in the Garden of Eden was an intimate relationship of co-laboring.

This is why He would be willing to give His life for us. And prayer is the conduit of conversation and relationship that brings us before the face of God.

Prayer is often reduced to something far less than relationship. Think about it. Many times, we can treat prayer as though it's only about our needs. But can you think of any other relationship in your life that is based only on one person's needs?

Prayer is the conduit of conversation and relationship that brings us before the face of God.

Or sometimes we treat prayer like it's a good luck charm. We throw up a prayer before a meal or before a significant event in our lives, hoping to invoke God's favor when we need it. But if we stop and think about it, that type of prayer doesn't sound like relationship. There is a different type of prayer, and that is prayer rooted in relationship with God.

David's response to God in Psalm 27 was a resolute "Your face, Lord, do I seek." There was something deep in his heart that responded to this invitation. And David had it all. He knew what it was like to have popularity, possessions and pleasures. But when he heard God say, "Seek My face," something deep within his inner being rose and responded.

I believe that we were all created for relationship with God, and each of us grope for fulfillment and satisfaction through other means. But we always end up back in the same place. It's not until we respond to this invitation from God to seek His face that the true longings of our hearts are fulfilled. Paul says this in Acts 17 when he's preaching in Athens. He says, "And He made from one man every nation of mankind to live on all the face of the earth, having determined allotted periods and the boundaries of their dwelling place, that they should seek God, and perhaps feel their way toward Him and find Him. Yet he is actually not far from each one of us."

This is why I place this truth at the top of the list as critical to a life of prayer. We must believe and understand that God doesn't just put up with us. Instead He created us for relationship with Him; therefore, prayer is essential to our existence. Prayer then moves from being an obligation to being a lifestyle. Learning to pray and experiencing prayer moves from being a response to guilt, to being a natural response to love.

Experience It

Confession

Pour you heart out to the Lord. Tell Him your struggles and the battles you're facing. Be honest and real with God.

Profession

Tell Him why you love Him and the things you're grateful for. Talk to Him about this fresh new season you desire of relationship with Him.

CHAPTER 2

Hide and Seek or Seek and Find?

Truth #2
God is not hard to find.

I love those who love Me,
and those who seek Me diligently find Me.
Proverbs 8:17

P rayer is a humble expression of a person's soul that responds to the reality that God wants relationship with us. Prayer is God's idea and not ours. It is not initiated by us; it's initiated by God.

This is vital to know and believe, because many times early in my own walk with Jesus, prayer was more of a wishful experiment. It was hard to know if God was listening, whether He cared or whether my prayers were 'doing the trick.' Then I encountered this truth spread throughout the Word of God: those who seek God will find Him (2 Chronicles 15:2, Psalm 34, Psalm 63:1 Proverbs 8:17, Jeremiah 29:13, Amos 5:4, Matthew 7:7, Acts 17:27).

I have four kids and I love our time together. We laugh, we wrestle, we play games, we love just being together. And like most fathers, I love to play hide and seek with my kids. But as a father, I am not playing to win. I am not thinking critically about how to find the most obscure spot or smallest unidentifiable space to somehow stump my 2-year-old. I want to be found. I find a place in the room where I am hidden out of plain site, yet easily found after some searching. The joy of a 2-year-old finding her father is filled with surprise, screams, shrieks and giggles. And the joy of a father is in the joy of his child.

If God wanted to, He could hide Himself from humanity so well that besides the evidence of His creative handiwork, there would be no revelation of who He is in our midst. But with a little searching, and with a little humility on our part, it is easy to recognize that not only does God want to be found, He has been the one continually pursuing us from the beginning. He didn't have to, but He did. He is the one who sets the stage for us to enter into a daily relationship of seeking Him.

"He came into the very world He created, but the world didn't recognize Him. He came to His own people, and even they rejected Him. But to all who believed Him and accepted Him, He gave the right to become children of God" (John 1:10-12). He pursued us. He initiated all of this. Therefore, prayer requires enough humility to respond to that with the response it deserves. The difference between those who seek Him and find Him, and those who seek Him and never find Him, is humility.

There is an age when kids think they are too cool for hide and seek (although none of my kids has come to it yet). They are figuring out the world, and finding their dad hiding behind a curtain doesn't have the same surprise factor it does for a preschooler. What very young children have is a simple wonder of the world around them, humility to enjoy the seeking and the finding. Any problems with prayer are on our side, not on God's. Prayer is about relationship (as we discovered in the first truth), not about feeding our pride, platform or popularity.

Any problems with prayer are on our side,
not on God's.

Jesus told the Pharisees, "You search the Scriptures because you think that in them you have eternal life; and it is they that bear witness about Me, yet you refuse to come to Me that you may have life" (John 5:39-40). They were searching, but they weren't finding. Why? They had pride or an agenda in their searching that kept them from God. Our pride blinds us from finding God. Their searching for the Savior or Messiah was in hopes of being on the right side of an argument. They were searching to solidify their positions of power in their culture.

James 4:6-8 says, "But He gives more grace. Therefore, it says, 'God opposes the proud but gives grace to the humble.' Submit yourselves therefore to God. Resist the devil, and he will flee from you. Draw near to God, and He will draw near to you." God loves to be found by us. He wouldn't have given His very best to redeem us if He didn't want to be found. Therefore, prayer is the grand conduit of love relationship with God—the thrill of seeking in desperation and dependence, and the pleasure of finding God and His eternally rich promises, presence and friendship. Seek Him and you will find Him.

Experience It

Confession

God, show me who You are. I want to know You. Take time to express your desire to seek after God.

Profession

Take time to ask God these two questions:

1. God, who are You?

2. God, who am I to You?

Calling Upon the Lord

Truth #3
Calling on God demonstrates dependence.

I call upon the Lord, who is worthy to be praised,
and I am saved from my enemies.
2 Samuel 22:4

My wife and I moved to the Seattle area after college. After a few years in the beautiful Northwest, Tanya and I began to feel the Lord was stirring us to move. But we had no idea what that meant. We had been working in the marketplace, paying off our debt and continuing our studies. I remember that season being characterized by a prayer that said, "Lord, wherever You want to take us, we'll go."

Over the months that followed, a number of opportunities came our way. We had an opportunity with Chi Alpha in Nebraska, and to minister to at-risk youth in our town in Washington. We also had a local church opportunity. Although these were great opportunities, none of them had that confirmation from God that we were waiting for.

After several months of this, we received a phone call from Iowa. At the time, we didn't know a soul in Iowa. The man on the other end of the line began describing an opportunity to come and start a Chi Alpha Campus Ministry at Iowa State University. Honestly, on the outside this opportunity was no better or worse than the others. But this open door had that peace from God that surpasses understanding. Ever since that experience, my wife and I have had a resolve to trust God with our lives. God answered our prayer and it has surpassed our expectations.

David was a teenager when he learned to depend on God. The people he loved, the Israelites, were facing an intimidating force in the Philistine army. And if they lost the battle, it would change the trajectory of the lives of his people for years to come. David heard about the challenge and a mighty faith welled up inside of him. This wasn't a faith in himself, it was a faith in God as his defender. He said, "The Lord who rescued me from the claws of the lion and the bear will rescue me from this Philistine" (1 Samuel 17:37).

David discovered the proper combination of God's strength and his obedience that made space for God to do the impossible. Interestingly David said, "Today the Lord will conquer you, and I will kill you and cut off your head." The battle is the Lord's, but God asks us to be a part of it. God conquered Goliath, and David killed Goliath. Prayer is not inaction. Prayer is the door to action in God's kingdom. Prayer is not passive; it makes room for God to move and then invites us to move with Spirit-empowered precision and faith.

As you fast forward through David's life, it is so encouraging that David didn't lose the dependence of his youth. David's battle against Goliath wasn't his only battle. One battle led to another, which led to another, each with lessons learned. He even faced the Philistines again. And apparently Goliath wasn't their only giant. There must have been something in the

Philistine's water because in 2 Samuel 22, David and his men killed four giants. David sang a song of praise saying, "The Lord is my rock, my fortress, and my savior; my God is my rock, in whom I find protection. He is my shield, the power that saves me, and my place of safety. He is my refuge, my savior, the one who saves me from violence. I *called upon the Lord*, who is worthy of praise, and He saved me from my enemies" (2 Samuel 22:2-4).

David was still willing and able to call upon the Lord, even in his later years. Calling upon the Lord is a declaration of our dependence on God as our defender, shield, protector and strength—the list goes on and on. For David, calling on God meant that he was giving God space to move on his behalf. Calling on God meant that David wasn't able in himself, so he humbly communicated his soul's true position of dependence.

This phrase "calling upon the Lord" was not unique to David. It was used a thousand years prior to describe the patriarchs' dependence on God. Abraham "called upon the Lord" after God told him to leave his country and go to a land that God would show him (Genesis 12). Abraham had to depend on

God. Jacob "called upon the Lord" after God provided him with fresh water in a new land (Genesis 26). Jacob had to depend on God. Moses "called upon the Lord" after God provided new tablets because the first had been destroyed during Israel's idolatrous distraction with the golden calf (Exodus 34). Moses had to depend on God.

> *God does not need to use us but He does want to use us.*

So David was following the example of great leaders before him. He recognized that in this kingdom of God, great things happened through dependence on God. Dependence made room for the impossible. I have grown convinced of this truth from Scripture. When people "called upon the Lord", their declared need for God made space for God to move His plan forward. When people did not "call upon the Lord", the favor and momentum of God's plan was halted. God does not *need* to use us, but He does *want* to use us. We, on the other hand, cannot do what God is calling us to do without leaning in and depending completely on God.

There are plenty of examples from Israel's history when they didn't call upon the Lord, but one vivid example stands out. After Joshua died in the promised land, there was a sense of contentment across the nation of Israel. There was a lack of awareness of the miraculous story they were a part of. The book of Judges says, "After that generation died, another generation grew up who did not acknowledge the Lord or remember the mighty things He had done for Israel." God's response to our stubbornness seems to be more a response of not defending, of letting us feel the natural consequences of life without His provision. The writer of Judges goes onto say, "He turned them over to their enemies all around, and they were no longer able to resist them. Every time Israel went out to battle, the Lord fought against them, causing them to be defeated, just as He had warned. And the people were in great distress."

Please don't misunderstand the character of God through this truth. God takes pleasure in providing for His children. He is not being cruel when He removes His hand of provision. He is simply giving us what our actions are communicating we want. When we don't call upon the Lord, we are saying we can do it on our own. But when we call upon the Lord, we are communicating through words and actions that we desperately need God to come through. We have stepped into unknown territory and we are completely dependent on God.

I'll point you back to the same passage I ended the first chapter with, Acts 17:26-28, "And He made from one man every nation of mankind to live on all the face of the earth, having determined allotted periods and the boundaries of their dwelling place, that they should seek God, and perhaps feel their way toward Him and find Him. Yet He is actually not far from each one of us, for 'In Him we live and move and have our being.'" He is not far from each one of us and He is our everything. I pray that each of us discovers that today in a new way.

Experience It

Confession
Take time to repent of any ways in which you have tried to fight battles on your own.

Profession
God is Savior and that means He is our only Savior. Declare His sufficiency to save you, redeem you and fight for you.

CHAPTER 4

Praying in the Name of Jesus

Truth #4
Jesus' Name is the way to the Father's heart.

Whatever you ask in My Name, this I will do,
that the Father may be glorified in the Son.
John 14:13

My father-in-law is a legend. His name is Cal Thompson, and he's one of those guys that have been faithful and fruitful over a lifetime. Not only has he been in ministry for more than 30 years, he has been in *youth* ministry for over 30 years, and 25 of those years in the same church. That's almost unheard of. For decades, he has gathered hundreds of middle- and high-school students and shared the good news of Jesus and his life.

My point is simply that Cal is a great man. Therefore, I find when I am in certain circles, that when I mention his name, it changes the whole conversation. Through the mention of his name, the excitement rises and stories come flowing out. I gain creditability or respect just for having a relationship with Cal.

I want to bring clarity to commonly used language in prayer. Believers often pray 'in Jesus' Name'. Why is that? Why do we continually mention Jesus' Name? Is that out of religious tradition, biblical obedience or what? There are a couple aspects of this I want us to understand.

First, Jesus Himself introduced this concept of praying in His Name. Not only did He say, "Whatever you ask in My Name...", He also prayed in His own Name when He prayed to the Father. In John 17:11b Jesus prays, "Holy Father, keep them in Your Name, which You have given Me, that they may be one, even as We are one." Jesus prays to His Father using the name the Father gave Him. There is such significance to this name that even Jesus Himself prays in His Name.

Jesus emphasizes praying in His Name. He says (more than once), "If you ask anything in My Name, it will be done for you" (John 14:13-14, John 15:16, John 16:23-26). Part of the power of praying in Jesus' Name is simple obedience. If Jesus tells us to pray in His Name, then we should do it. Jesus came and introduced a kingdom. In this kingdom, King Jesus gives us ways of doing things, and this is one of those things. I encourage you, as you discover Jesus' commands in the Word, that you step into simple and immediate obedience. That's the best response. We don't need to understand the why before we obey. Instead, oftentimes, it's *after* we obey that we begin to understand the why.

That being said, I want to emphasize the logical power of Jesus' Name aside from the straightforward commands of Jesus. When I mention the name of my father-in-law, I am seeking to gain approval, creditability or relationship with the people around me. That's the raw, honest truth. If we remember that prayer is a simple conversation with God, then the

Name of Jesus becomes the pathway to approval, credibility and relationship with the Father.

Praying in Jesus' Name is a constant reminder of God's grace poured out to us through Jesus.

Jesus said, "No one comes to the Father except through Me" (John 14:6). He is our way to the heart of the Father. When we pray in Jesus' Name, the Father sees the righteousness of Christ. When we pray in Jesus' Name, the Father sees the authority of Christ. When we pray in Jesus' Name, the Father perks up simply because Jesus is His only begotten Son. Praying in Jesus' Name is not a magic trick or formula. When we think of it in terms of relationship, then praying in Jesus' Name is a conscious reminder of God's grace poured out to us through Jesus. The only reason we can come to the Father is because of Jesus.

On top of this, it's important to understand the significance of a name from the perspective of Jesus' first century, primarily Jewish audience. To them, a person's name was much more than just a title given to them by their parents. For Jesus' audience, a name represented the entirety of who someone was. It included their reputation, their character, their territory, and so on. Therefore, when He says, "If you ask anything in My Name...", He is telling them they have the authority to invoke all that Jesus is—His perfect reputation, perfect character and unquestioned territory.

Praying in Jesus' Name is therefore a conscious declaration that we come into God's presence because of Jesus. It's that banner over our lives that gives us everything we need for life in God. I'll end this chapter with this simple, yet inexhaustible verse. Ephesians 1:3 says, "Blessed be the God and Father of our Lord Jesus Christ, who has blessed us in Christ with every spiritual blessing in the heavenly places." In Christ we are blessed with everything we need when we come before the Father in these heavenly places of prayer and petition. I pray this prayer over each one of you.

Experience It

Confession

Confess ways in which you have lowered the value of the Name of Jesus.

Profession

Take extended time to exalt Jesus' Name as the Name above all names.

CHAPTER 5

Our Authority in Christ

Truth #5
Prayer is our place of authority as believers.

Let us then with confidence draw near to the
throne of grace, that we may receive mercy and
find grace to help in time of need.
Hebrews 4:16

I remember the day like yesterday. My boss called
me into his office, handed me a piece of paper
and said, "Congratulations Drew, you can go and
pick up your white helmet." There was more to the
conversation, but that's the part that mattered. I had
fulfilled the requirements, and now I was officially a
journeyman engineer. On the surface, the only thing

that changed was the color of my helmet. Entry-level engineers wore green helmets, and journeyman engineers wore white helmets. But earning that white helmet meant that now I had greater responsibilities and authority.

Generally, authority is supposed to match a certain competency in an area. It's usually meant to match up with a position's level of impact. Authority is critical to effectiveness. Authority in this world largely hinges on positions, and authority in the Kingdom of Jesus hinges on position as well. The difference is that worldly positions are attained through personal experience, education, credentials or even nepotism. In the Kingdom of God, a position of authority is attained through Jesus' perfect experience, perfect knowledge, perfect credentials and because we are His children, made perfect through Him. That combination sets us up for massive positional authority and responsibility in the Kingdom of God.

Imagine you started your first day at a new job. You begin working in your cubicle, doing paperwork, answering emails and getting situated, when your boss calls you into his or her office. Your boss says, "Congratulations, you can go and pick up your white helmet." You don't know how to respond. You haven't done anything to earn it. You don't feel qualified. You don't feel competent. Your boss can tell you don't know how to respond so he or she gives you an explanation, "I am granting you a position of great authority, not because of what you have done, but because of what I have done. You see, I have an 'open door' policy to all who work here and you have 100% access to my qualifications."

The Kingdom of God is like this; the credentials necessary to come before the Father are astronomical. On our own we have zero authority. As we look at the Old Testament, we quickly see that God is holy and we are not. We recognize that even our best is like filthy rags before God. But Jesus flipped the script of the Old Testament by fulfilling all of the requirements of the Old Covenant. He did this not just to show that it could be done, but to then take our place and satisfy the requirements on our behalf.

The good news of Jesus is so good because He made a way for us, not just to avoid punishment, but to be contributors and participants in this amazing Kingdom. In Jesus' Kingdom, He says, "All authority in heaven and on earth has been given to Me. Go, therefore and make disciples of all nations" (Matthew 28:18b-19a). He lets us share in His authority. And one of the primary positions of influence and action in the Kingdom of Jesus is in prayer.

> *The good news of Jesus is so good because He made a way for you and I, not just to avoid punishment, but to be contributors and participants in this amazing Kingdom.*

In prayer, we can come before God with a bold confidence. This bold confidence does not hinge on anything we have done; it has nothing to do with our credentials. Instead, it hinges completely on Jesus and, as we already talked about, Jesus is sufficient.

Hebrews 4:14-16 says, "Since then we have a great high priest who has passed through the heavens, Jesus, the Son of God, let us hold fast our confession. For we do not have a high priest who is unable to sympathize with our weaknesses, but One who in every respect has been tempted as we are, yet without sin. Let us then with confidence draw near to the throne of grace, that we may receive mercy and find grace to help in time of need."

This passage is so powerful because it illuminates the access we have to lay ourselves bare before God. We do not need to put on any sort of show or performance. Our authority has nothing to do with that. Not only that, but Jesus is ultimately familiar with the pressures and brokenness of our world. He faced it, yet was perfect. We can have bold confidence to throw ourselves before the throne of grace, where we'll receive the precise authority we need to move forward with God's will in our lives.

Our world leaves us feeling massively insecure. From the day we are born, we grope and long for acceptance and approval from people. We go in and out of seasons of confidence based on worldly standards. Some days we feel like we are doing great, and other days we feel like we lagging behind. We can work hard and still we won't measure up according to everyone's standards.

But, the Kingdom of Jesus is so different and I want each of us to catch that. The more and more people discover their authority in prayer through Jesus, the more effective we will be. I am excited to watch a generation of people discover a place of rest in the authority of Jesus. I am excited for us to understand the influence and 'open door policy' that Christ gives us. That's what changes the world.

Experience It

Confession

Confess your insecurities to the Lord. Take time to submit your significance and value fully to God.

Profession

Thank Jesus for the authority He has given to you. Take time to speak out loud about the confident boldness that the throne room of grace has granted you.

CHAPTER 6

If We Really Believe...

Truth #6
Faith rests in what we know about God's
character and His promises.

You can pray for anything,
and if you have faith, you will receive it.
Matthew 21:22

Faith is the currency of the Kingdom of God.
The currency of the world we live in is power,
position and possessions. Even a small amount
of faith in the kingdom of God can be extremely significant. People in this world can admire faith and
value it to an extent, but they don't value it as much
as compared to other things. The real value of faith is
in the Kingdom of God. There is a tremendously fa-
vorable exchange rate when we pass faith through the

work of Jesus' cross and resurrection. Faith then exalts the God of the impossible as Lord and master over a situation.

Jesus said you can pray for anything, and if you have faith, you will receive it. Faith is the key ingredient to that statement having any power or substance to it. Faith is the common denominator of much of the healing Jesus demonstrated in His ministry. The gospels record Jesus saying, "Your faith has made you well" time and time again (Matthew 9:22, Mark 10:52, Luke 5:50, Luke 17:19, Luke 18:42). Other times Jesus emphasized that in the Kingdom of God it is done "in accordance with your faith" (Matthew 9:29, Matthew 15:28, Matthew 21:21).

When it came to Jesus' inner circle, there were several times He helped them realize their "little faith" was a hindrance to them in the Kingdom. He gave them insight into the Kingdom He was bringing to earth. In the Kingdom of Jesus, faith is trust in God's character and promises. In one instance, Jesus is walking on water and Peter gets out of the boat and walks on the water too. Once Peter takes his eyes off Jesus though, he begins to sink. Jesus immediately stretches out His hand and grabs Peter, and His response is extremely insightful. He says, "O, you of little faith, why did you doubt?" I don't believe Jesus could have a condescending tone. I believe He was genuinely helping Peter understand that there was literally no reason to doubt, and the reason he sank was his lack of faith.

In that moment standing on the waves, Peter began to trust his own natural instincts, and he began to give credence to the doubts in his own mind. God was already doing the impossible. Peter was defying the laws of physics by walking on water, yet his doubts had a power over him that took the place of faith. I believe when Jesus stretched out His hand to grab Peter and spoke to him, the tone in His voice was overflowing with love. He could see Peter's destiny as a man of great faith. This was a moment for Peter to know that Jesus can be trusted, even when it seems impossible.

Life is filled with opportunities to trust our own instincts instead of the character and promises of God. This is the difference between doubt and faith. The truth is, we do not know best. God does. He is faithful and His promises are true.

A few years ago, I walked through a season of doubts and anxiety as I was pastoring the Chi Alphas across Iowa. I had recently experienced several blows in ministry that left me feeling completely alone and defeated. I had never dealt with anxiety before. I was generally a pretty low-stress guy. But something about those trials left me questioning and doubting. I am extremely thankful for several individuals in my life during that period, but specifically I had a Christian counselor that helped me a lot.

Besides just giving me an outlet to talk things out, this counselor equipped me with several tools to help me think about what is true. He taught me to use labels in my mind to categorize what is untrue and what is true. So when I have a thought that says, "I am all alone." I can label that for what it is and replace it with truth: that Jesus said He will never leave me nor forsake me. When I feel like I don't measure up, I can quickly label that as untrue. Living with faith then becomes a conscious choice of believing and thinking on what is true. This may seem simplistic, but I challenge you to place yourself in Peter's position walking on the water. In that moment, faith meant believing what was right in front of him (Jesus). Doubt, on the other hand, meant believing what was all around him and even underneath him. Doubt meant believing what seemed logical (that people can't walk on water), while faith meant believing Jesus' promise (that Peter could walk on water because of Jesus).

We are given a definition of faith in Hebrews 11:1 "Now faith is the assurance of things hoped for, the conviction of things not seen." It is an assurance and a conviction—an assurance in promises, and a conviction about who God is. The writer of Hebrews then goes through much of the redemptive story, highlighting the role of faith throughout. Faith is the currency of the Kingdom of God.

We see that the great men and women of faith in God's story had an assurance in the promises that God had given them. There were promises of an inheritance (Hebrews 11:8), promises of a land (Hebrews 11:9), promises of a child (Hebrews 11:11), promises of provision (Hebrews 11:17), promises of future blessing (Hebrews 11:20) and promises of a coming freedom (Hebrews 11:22). They also demonstrated a conviction about who God is. They knew God as all-powerful Creator of the universe (Hebrews 11:3), He is holy (Hebrews 11:4), He is righteous judge

(Hebrews 11:7), He is designer and builder (Hebrews 11:10), He is faithful (Hebrews 11:11) and He is able (Hebrews 11:19).

And it's from the testimonies of the greats from biblical history that the writer of Hebrews points to Jesus as the author and perfecter of our faith. It says, "Therefore, since we are surrounded by so great a cloud of witnesses, let us also lay aside every weight, and sin which clings so closely, and let us run with endurance the race that is set before us, looking to Jesus, the founder and perfecter of our faith, who for the joy that was set before Him endured the cross, despising the shame, and is seated at the right hand of the throne of God."

We are blessed to live in a day when we can have more faith than even the faith of the greats, because we have Jesus.

Sin tangles us up and distracts us from running unhindered after what God has for us. And as we look at Jesus, we find both the conception of our faith and the perfection of our faith. We are blessed to live in a day when we can have more faith than even the faith of the greats, because we have Jesus. He sits at the righthand of the throne of God; He has accomplished victory over the enemy and purchased us right standing with the Father.

We can have a burning conviction about the character of God because Jesus and the Father are one. If we see Jesus, we have seen the Father (John 14:9). We can have a greater faith because we have a greater revelation of what God is like. We can also have an assurance of many great and precious promises. The Word of God is filled with promises that can empower us to run our race with endurance.

Jesus tells us, "You can pray for anything, and if you have faith, you will receive it" (Matthew 21:22). You can know that is true when you fully understand what faith is rooted in. Faith, properly understood, is never disappointed. Faith is grounded in conviction of God's character and assurance of His promises; therefore, if you pray for anything out of a conviction and assurance of God's ways, you WILL receive it. You can be confident in it. You can take it to the bank. Faith is the currency of the Kingdom.

Experience It

Confession

Ask God to show you any areas of your life you struggle to believe Him for and ask Him to show you who He is in that area. For example, if you have trouble having faith in the area of finances, ask God to show you He is the God of generosity. If you have trouble believing you're forgiven of sin, ask God to show you He is the God of grace.

Profession

Take time to build your faith by declaring His consistent character. Then take time to declare His promises over your life and situations in your life.

CHAPTER 7

Persistent Prayer

Truth #7
God rewards persistence.

*So don't you think God will surely give justice to His
chosen people who cry out to Him day and night?
Will He keep putting them off?
I tell you, He will grant justice to them quickly!*
Luke 18:7-8

O n one hand, there is a mystery to prayer that
we will never understand. The fact that God
would choose to give us the opportunity to
co-labor with Him in regards to the most important
things in this world, is hard to wrap my mind around.
On the other hand, there are promises we are given
regarding prayer. It's important that we take those
promises and believe them.

Jesus tells a parable about a widow who keeps coming before the judge in her city to plead her case. Jesus tells us that she has an adversary. It must be pretty rough, because she is relentless in crying out for help and mercy from the judge. The problem is that the judge is not a good judge. Jesus says he is an unjust judge. Specifically, the judge doesn't care about God's opinion or care about people. That's a tough situation for the widow. Trying to get help from an unjust judge is like trying to get help from a doctor who doesn't care about people or help from a car mechanic that doesn't care about fixing the car. Judges are meant to bring justice and this judge wasn't good at that.

But this woman was persistent. It's a parable, so it's not meant to have a backstory or tremendous detail. It's meant to communicate a truth about the Kingdom of God. This woman was in a desperate situation though, and she saw this judge as her only hope. So she did what she could and "kept coming to him." Eventually he is so bothered by her, that he decides to give her justice. It wasn't because he cared about her, or because she presented a compelling case, it was because she was 'bothering' him. He relented and gave her justice.

Jesus reveals an important truth with this extreme story that I hope we catch. He asks, "So don't you think God will surely give justice to His chosen people who cry out to Him day and night?" If we think of ourselves as the widow who is in a desperate situation, and God as our judge, nothing changes on our end of the equation. God is our only hope; we have nowhere else to go. But on God's end, pretty much everything changes. Unlike the judge in the story, God *is* just and God *does* care about His people. Here He calls us His "chosen people." So, in light of this story, we can be confident that God answers the persistent prayer of His people. Luke actually tells us the point of the parable before Jesus even says it. Luke said, "One day Jesus told His disciples a story to show that they should always pray and never give up."

There is an aspect of prayer that needs to be persistent. I am not sure why, but it's a truth that I recognize. There is truth and mystery here. Truth in the promise of "God giving us justice", but mystery in why God doesn't just give us the answer right away. There seems to be a paradox at work because Jesus even says, "He will bring us justice quickly", but the whole point to the parable is persistence. Persistence implies that it's not instant.

One of the greatest men of prayer I know is my father. Growing up, my dad would often talk of the value of prayer. He wouldn't try to get philosophical about it, but would say something very similar to what was described in the story here. My dad would say, "I am not sure what we should do about..., but I know we need to pray." My dad would often push me towards prayer. And he had a way of saying it that carried weight with me. It didn't sound preachy or cliché. Trust me, I have seen many refrigerator magnets, placards and t-shirts that said something like "pray and don't give up." But when my father said it, it was different.

There is a big difference between hearing words that are true and experiencing the truth of those words. I believe my dad's words carried more weight later in life because I saw his persistence in prayer and the fruit of that persistence. My dad would talk about how our local church was "built on prayer." He spent a lot of time praying there. Saturday morning and Sunday evenings, I have many memories of watching my dad on his knees. My dad would talk very honestly about not knowing what to do in a situation, but he knew he could pray. I saw him many times at his bedside, crying out to God for our family, his marriage, for the miraculous.

Sometimes we can allow the mystery of prayer to keep us away from the power of prayer.

And here's the reality: in my dad's testimony, persistence did not equal instant answers. My father walked through numerous difficult seasons, but he persisted in prayer. The fruit is evident today in his life, family and ministry, and in the miracles he is surrounded by. Sometimes we can allow the mystery of prayer to keep us away from the power of prayer. Let's not let that be the case for us.

Experience It

Confession

Reflect on battles you gave up praying for. Give those
things back to the Lord.

Profession

Meditate on God as the One who loves justice and
mercy. Declare His power and desire to bring justice
to the situations you are facing.

CHAPTER 8

A Desperate Faith

Truth #8
God uses desperate people.

*Blessed are those who hunger and thirst
for righteousness, for they shall be satisfied.*
Matthew 5:6

I venture to say that desperation is not seen as a positive thing. Think about a desperate situation. Maybe you find yourself in a desperate situation now. Desperate situations are categorized by discomfort to the degree that it seems there is little to no hope. Desperation can be the result of our own action or inaction, the actions of others, or just the consequence of natural events. Whichever it is, desperation is usually seen as a negative thing.

This is a difficult chapter to write because I never want to seem insensitive to the reality of anyone's suffering. I am a pastor, meaning God has called me to live in the trenches with people facing serious issues. I am not a philosopher or a theologian—I am a pastor. I seek to unpack the Word of God, specifically the good news of Jesus, in a way that is relevant to our lives. I hope you can trust me as I unpack this truth and try to open your heart to the power of desperation.

Matthew, Mark and Luke all tell the story of a man that was paralyzed and desperate to be healed by Jesus. Jesus was in a house in Capernaum, teaching and demonstrating the Kingdom by healing the sick. The house was jam-packed and the crowd flowed out into the streets. There was no way this guy could get in to see Jesus today. He was too late. He missed his chance.

But who knows if this would be his only chance? What if Jesus moved on from Capernaum that day and he missed his only opportunity? This man had heard reports of Jesus healing other paralytics and the blind, and even a report of Jesus casting out demons. This paralyzed man, who was confined to his bed, knew this was his moment of hope. Desperation welled up in his soul, and it pushed him out of the box of what is normal and expected.

The man rallied four of his friends. He knew these men loved him enough to help him. The problem was, he didn't have much of a plan. This paralyzed man convinced his four friends to stop at nothing to get him before Jesus. If he could get just 30 seconds before this Messianic Healer, he knew his life could be forever changed. One of his friends spoke up with a bold idea, 'The roof! What if we lower him through the roof?' The idea seemed better than the other ideas of yelling 'fire' or trying to convince the crowd to bodysurf their friend to Jesus. So the group of four friends carried this man with growing faith to the roof.

These friends went for it. They start disassembling the roof and soon they could see the tops of peoples' heads below. They could hear the voice of Jesus, and they could see Him healing others. After several minutes of taking apart somebody's roof, there was enough room to lower this paralytic man's bed down right in front of Jesus. And they did just that. The Bible says, "And when Jesus saw their faith" (Mark 2:5).

That's right, Jesus saw their faith. Their faith had grown and grown to a place of utter desperation, so much so that it became visible through action. Needless to say, Jesus healed this faith-filled, desperate man—his life forever changed by the power of Jesus.

> *Desperation grows into faith, seeing Jesus not as a generic miracle worker, but as your personal miracle worker.*

Desperation is a growing response to a seemingly hopeless situation. It starts with the realization that the situation is not going to change without a miracle. Without God's divine intervention, the situation seems hopeless. From that admission, the desperation grows towards faith, seeing Jesus not just as a generic miracle worker, but as *your* personal miracle worker. You begin to see Jesus differently. You see who He is and realize that His consistent character is worth trusting. From there, desperate faith leads to action. At that point, there seems to be nothing you won't do to express that faith to Jesus.

Desperation > Desperate faith > Faith-filled action

In the stories about Jesus, there are many that fit this description. Consider the woman with the issue of blood, who had spent the last of her money on doctors with no results. She pushed through the crowd and thought, if I can just touch His robe... Or there's the account of the blind man that won't stop shouting for Jesus. The crowd is telling him to be quiet; he is starting to lose his voice, but he knows this is his only hope. He cries out and Jesus has mercy on him and heals him. And the stories go on and on. Desperation can lead to faith, which can lead to faith-filled action.

On a weekly basis, I spend time with individuals and families that face desperate situations. These situations break my heart. And if I'm not careful, they can weigh on me. Marital difficulties, mental illness, kids that have walked away from God, physical pain that people have endured for decades, each situation carrying a desperation of its own. However, (and I say this with the compassion of a pastor) it breaks my heart when people don't allow their desperation to push them towards a desperate faith. In fact, many times they allow their desperation to do the opposite. Their desperation leads them to come up with unbiblical explanations for their situation. Or they allow their desperation to isolate them from their community and those who love them most. They can also allow their desperation to give a foothold to bitterness or resentment.

I want to see this change in our church. I want to hear the cry of people that are desperate for God to move in their lives. I want to see what happens when our desperate situations lead to desperate faith, which swells to faith-filled action. From a biblical standpoint, the precedent is solid. Jesus said that in His Kingdom, the hungry and thirsty are blessed because they will be satisfied (Matthew 5:6). I want us to discover this desperate faith.

Experience It

Confession
Confess your desperation to the Lord. Admit that without Him, there is no hope.

Profession
As your desperation grows, cry out to God declaring your faith in His sole power to change your situation/life.

CHAPTER 9

Breakthrough Prayer

Truth #9
Breakthrough is ours in Jesus.

Then the Lord gave special strength to Elijah.
1 Kings 18:46

A s you stare at the eastern horizon early in the morning, before the sun has come up, there is darkness all around you. The stars still fill the sky. The morning is still crisp and cool. Then it happens: the eastern sky gradually starts to warm with shades of pink and orange until breakthrough happens. The sun breaks the horizon and a new day arrives. Now the momentum of the day is underway, and the sky illuminates at an exponential rate. This is breakthrough.

Breakthrough is one of the main reasons we pray. It is the moment when a situation changes, a heart is softened, cancer is healed, a financial drought is over or when a family is redeemed. Not all prayers are requesting a breakthrough. There are prayers of thanksgiving, prayers of confession or prayers of declaration. But when it comes to prayers of faith, intercession or healing, breakthrough is the reward.

Breakthrough is what Jesus promised in Matthew 7:7, "Ask, and it will be given to you; seek, and you will find; knock, and it will be opened to you." Or, in John 14:13-14, "Whatever you ask in My Name, this I will do, that the Father may be glorified in the Son. If you ask Me anything in My Name, I will do it." Or as the apostle John said, "And this is the confidence that we have toward Him, that if we ask anything according to His will, He hears us. And if we know that He hears us in whatever we ask, we know that we have the requests that we have asked of Him." Or as James wrote, "The prayer of a righteous person has great power as it is working."

But is breakthrough always a distant hope? Is it an intangible belief in a promise? Or is it obvious and inarguable? Based on Scripture, I contend that there is a moment of breakthrough as we pray and it is evident in one of two ways (and many times both): 1) a tangible faith of *knowing* breakthrough happened and 2) physical evidence in the natural world around us.

James 5:17-18 says, "Elijah was a man with a nature like ours, and he prayed fervently that it might not rain, and for three years and six months it did not rain on the earth. Then he prayed again, and heaven gave rain, and the earth bore its fruit." James summarizes an epic Old Testament account of breakthrough prayer. And James references Elijah not just to validate his place in God's redemptive story, but to give each of us hope in our prayers that sometimes seem bigger than we have faith for.

James is referencing the story in 1 Kings 18, which tells of Elijah's prayer to end the drought in Israel. In verse 42, it says, "Elijah climbed to the top of Mount Caramel bowed low to the ground and prayed with his face between his knees." Elijah needed breakthrough. He hiked to a position where he could see his breakthrough and he prayed intensely. After a little while, Elijah tells his servant, "Go and look for the rain clouds." His servant does it, but quickly returns and says, "I didn't see anything." Elijah does this seven times.

This story often comes back to life for me while I'm praying. I experience an ebb and flow between faith and reality—between what I know to be true in God's Word, and what I think I see with my eyes. But Elijah didn't let that stop him. He knew breakthrough was coming. He kept praying and he kept watching, praying and watching, praying and watching—seven times in all. I imagine his servant grew weary. I wonder if his servant thought this great prophet had finally lost it. Maybe the stress of taking on 450 prophets of Baal took its toll on Elijah and he finally cracked. Maybe Elijah lost what he once had.

But it's so funny the lies that float around in our minds when we are diligently seeking something significant in prayer. All of those lies hinge on the idea that what made Elijah great was Elijah himself. But it was never Elijah in the first place that raised the widow's son from the dead. Elijah wasn't able to provide food for himself during the drought; instead God fed him from the mouths of ravens. Elijah was never a great prophet because of himself. So why would that change now? Elijah was resolute and knew breakthrough was coming because he knew the God he was crying out to.

Finally the seventh time came. Elijah prayed and told his servant to go and look again. This time his servant returned and said he saw a "little cloud the size of a man's hand rising from the sea." You read that correct, the servant saw a cloud the size of a man's hand. I don't know that I have ever seen a cloud that small. But Elijah saw that physical evidence as the sign of breakthrough. He knew rain was coming. Elijah had so much faith in this breakthrough, that he told his servant to go right away and tell the wicked, unbelieving King Ahab the news. That's faith.

The breakthrough happened for Elijah at the moment there was a glimmer of physical evidence, and it was accompanied by a faith that Elijah didn't need to be convinced of. God gave him breakthrough in two ways: 1) physical evidence (although it was small) and 2) faith to recognize it. Therefore, when we pray, we can ask and believe that God will give us the breakthrough we need.

But realize that oftentimes, our breakthrough in prayer happens prior to the actual answer to prayer. Elijah knew God was beginning the work of sending rain when he saw the tiny cloud and commanded his servant to spread the word. I have noticed in my own life, that I will pray for something in accordance with the Scripture we read above (Matthew 7:7 or John 14:13-14), and eventually something will change outwardly. The tone of the relationship changes, physically something small changes, a humbling sense of God's presence comes, or I'm given a peace that surpasses understanding. Each of these seemingly small signs may be the breakthrough, if I have the faith to recognize them.

Lately, one of my most consistent prayers is for my own kids. I spend a lot of time praying that my kids will love Jesus with all that they are. I pray their faith and passion will surpass mine and Tanya's. I am realizing that I need to recognize the moments of breakthrough God gives me in that prayer.

The final answer to that request won't be realized for decades. But, in the meantime, I need to recognize "the tiny cloud" the Lord has sent, and respond in faith. When I watch my kids worshiping with a song to Jesus, that is a breakthrough. When one of my kids responds to another child in mercy, that is a breakthrough. When my son says he enjoyed seeking

God together at the altar at church, that is a breakthrough. When my daughter shares the love of Jesus with her classmate, that is a breakthrough. I need to recognize all of these breakthroughs.

How often do we miss the breakthrough because we squander what we are given?

Elijah was given a small sign, a cloud the size of his hand, and his faith recognized it as breakthrough. This is faith-filled stewardship. Stewardship is the mindset of the Kingdom that, in faith, makes the most of what we are given. How often do we miss the breakthrough because we squander what we are given? How often do we lack the gratitude or faith to recognize the seed of what's to come?

I believe God will give us eyes to see what He is doing. This requires a faith to believe that God is the God of breakthrough. God only calls us to things bigger than us. If we could do them in our own power, we would have no need for Him. God calls us to things that we could never do in our own power, and as we go after these things, God will give us eyes to recognize His breakthrough and steward it to the end.

Experience It

Confession

A major part of breakthrough is stewarding what He has already given us. Confess any ways in which you may have missed what He is doing in your life.

Profession

Declare God as the God of breakthrough. Declare dependence and trust in His power to do the miraculous. Declare the ways in which He has shown His power in the past, and ask Him to show you the breakthroughs you may have missed.

CHAPTER 10

A Corporate Sound

> **Truth #10**
> Some purposes in prayer are only
> accomplished when we pray as one.

*If My people who are called by My Name humble
themselves, and pray and seek My face...*
2 Chronicles 7:14

I loved playing sports with my dad and brothers growing up. In my earlier years, my dad would sometimes voluntarily play with a handicap. He would bat one-handed in baseball or shoot free throws with his eyes closed, or be all-time quarterback for both teams, with hopes of leveling the playing field. Sadly, I believe that our church has been *unintentionally* living with a handicap that holds us back and levels the playing field (in some senses) with the enemy.

Up until this point in the book, I have been emphasizing individual prayer—prayer between you and God. But one aspect of prayer that cannot be denied is prayer that God calls us to together. Some of God's purposes are only accomplished when His people join together in an intentional way.

This was the most difficult chapter to write for a few reasons. First, we live in such an individualistic culture that to talk about things only accomplished by a group seems foreign to us. Our minds don't easily grapple with ideas centered around community life together. We aren't used to admitting we need other people. Second, corporate prayer adds to the mystery of the power of prayer. In a prior chapter, I talked about the mystery of persistence. When we pray, there is much that we will never understand because God is working in the unseen. So if we begin talking about prayer together as a church, the mystery is only multiplied. Finally, we live in an age that does not cater to slowing down and praying together. Praying with others requires something of our calendars, and people feel like they are busier than ever before.

Even though this chapter was a challenge to write, I had to push forward. The reason I was determined to write on corporate prayer (when a church family prays together) is that throughout Scripture there is a clear pattern of God using group prayer to accomplish His work in the church and in the world.

It's important to remember that the good news of Jesus is a message of personal response into a community of believers. No one can decide to follow Jesus for you. And our affiliations or family heritage are not sufficient in maintaining a meaningful relationship with God. Instead, that relationship is discovered only through personal encounter with Jesus. But as soon as that miraculous exchange happens, we are brought into something much bigger than any one of us. We are brought into the Body of Christ.

Together we embody the life, power, and most importantly, the love of Jesus in this world. We cannot do that alone. We do it together. The New Testament is flooded with examples of the effectiveness of corporate prayer. In Acts 2, the church is born because of what God poured out upon a gathering of 120 believers. They encountered something together that turned a world upside down.

In Acts 4, we find one of the greatest accounts of a corporate prayer gathering. The church gathered and prayed together to seek God for breakthrough in the persecution they were facing. "After this prayer, the meeting place shook, and they were all filled with the Holy Spirit" (Acts 4:31a). In Acts 12, it was the prayer of the church that led to Peter's miraculous escape from prison. "While Peter was in prison, the church prayed very earnestly for him" (Acts 12:5). In Acts 13, a number of people gather in prayer and, in that gathering, God commissions Paul and Barnabas to be sent out as missionaries. It's the combined prayer of Paul and Silas in a prison cell that shakes the entire prison free, and creates a way for the prison guard and his family to encounter Jesus.

I could go on and on with examples from Scripture, but we oftentimes miss these examples because we tend to read Scripture through an individualistic lens. We read the Old Testament stories of God raising up and using *a people* as a metaphor for our individual need for Jesus. We read the New Testament stories and letters of God raising up *a people* to represent Him on the earth through the lens of personally fleshing out our daily walk with Jesus. Like I said, the individual response is necessary, but it's always an individual response that leads us into something bigger than any one of us.

I believe our church has been trying to fight our battles with our hands tied behind our backs. We have been trying to shoot free throws with our eyes closed. We have been unintentionally making it easier for the enemy because we all try to fight our battles solo. What if God created us for something more? What if we read God's Word through the lens of what He created us for as the Body of Christ, and realized that life together (including our prayer life) is better than life on our own.

> *I believe our church has been trying to fight our battles with our hands tied behind our backs.*

God invited us into something together when He spoke to Israel thousands of years ago. He said in 2 Chronicles 7:14-16, "If My people who are called by My Name humble themselves, and pray and seek My face and turn from their wicked ways, then I will hear from heaven and will forgive their sin and heal their land. Now My eyes will be open and My ears attentive to the prayer that is made in this place. For now I have chosen and consecrated this house that My Name may be there forever. My eyes and My heart will be there for all time." He says "If my people." That means the promise is contingent on our collective response.

In these verses, Solomon had just completed and dedicated the temple. This was a major feat that was passed down to him from his father, and God gives this clearer picture of His intentions for the temple. God intended the temple to be a place where His presence dwelt with such reality that righteousness, forgiveness and healing were truly experienced in peoples' lives. As we fast forward, all of this is fulfilled in Jesus. We don't have a temple today, because Jesus tore the veil of separation and made it possible for us to come into His presence, and for His presence to dwell in each one of us. But even that description misses part of the power of what Jesus actually came and accomplished.

Ephesians 2:19-22 says, "So then you are no longer strangers and aliens, but you are fellow citizens with the saints and members of the household of God, built on the foundation of the apostles and prophets, Christ Jesus Himself being the cornerstone, in whom the whole structure, being joined together, grows into a holy temple in the Lord. In Him you also are being built together into a dwelling place for God by the Spirit."

Paul says we grow together and become a holy temple in the Lord. According to Paul's description here, God's presence is hosted in us collectively as believers in a similar way as the Old Testament temple hosted the presence of God. We are each a brick in the wall of the temple. There are some things in God we cannot experience alone. We are created for community, and that's not just something churches say to get people to 'get with the program.' There is a Scriptural foundation to the reality that God expresses some things only to a group of people working together.

Consider this real-world example. Imagine you are moving to a new house. You could move some of your boxes and small furniture alone, but it's going to take a long time. It would be so much easier if you had some help. But there comes a time in moving when you cannot do it on your own, no matter how much time you have. No matter how strong you are and how long you work at it, you cannot move your piano without another person to help you. I believe it is similar with prayer. There are some things in life that can be accomplished through personal prayer. Other things are of such magnitude that many are needed.

We are each a brick in the wall of the temple. There are some things in God we cannot experience alone.

Therefore, in the days ahead, I see a church that takes God's Word seriously and truly believes that our prayer together matters. I see a church like the church in the book of Acts where "They all met together and were constantly united in prayer" (Acts 1:14 NLT). I see a church that will stop battling the enemy with a handicap. I see a church that will equip itself to take new ground for Jesus in our city and in our world. This will only be done through prayer together.

Experience It

Confession

Give God time to speak to you about our church. God may want to use you to stir up our community to contend for specific things.

Profession

Make a commitment before the Lord about joining with others in prayer.

CHAPTER 11

What if Prayer Is Boring?

> **Truth #11**
> Prayer is action in the Kingdom.

So, could you not watch with Me one hour?
Watch and pray that you may not enter into temptation.
Matthew 26:40-41

I am often reminded of the verse above when I pray. Like anyone else, and like the disciples, I find myself sometimes distracted, sleepy or bored in prayer. What do I do with that? Should I feel bad about that? Or should I give up, and expect that to always be the case? I want to address the humanity of our prayer.

Jesus comes back from an intense time of prayer with the Father, only to find His disciples asleep. He wakes them and asks them this question, "So, could you not watch with Me one hour?" I don't believe that Jesus was condemning his disciples and saying, 'You good-for-nothings, you can't even pray for one hour?' It's not that Jesus would never speak frankly, but I believe Jesus was looking to get the disciples' attention. He was calling them to recognize what they were falling victim to, and what was at stake.

In the next sentence, Jesus says, "The spirit indeed is willing, but the flesh is weak." Jesus reveals the dynamic at work when we pray. The truth is, prayer is action in the Kingdom of Jesus. Prayer is where things happen. Mountains are moved. Lives are changed. God is given room to do what only He can do. Situations are changed. Bodies are healed. Relationships are restored. The miraculous is initiated. Because the Spirit of God lives in us, we know this to be true. And that is why the spirit is willing. I believe each of us desires to engage in a level and intensity of prayer that aligns with what's at stake.

At the same time, there is such power in what Jesus reveals, because we must recognize our flesh as a real part of the equation. There is power in calling it like it is. We don't have to pretend our flesh away. Our flesh is real. And it's our humanity that draws us towards boredom, distractions and sleepiness in prayer. That's our flesh. Our spirit is willing, but our flesh is weak.

Therefore, Jesus combines two words that I hope stick with each of us. He says, "Watch and pray." There is nothing passive or boring about that phrase. That word 'watch' means "to be on the alert." It is the very opposite of being bored or distracted. He calls us to pray with our spiritual eyes wide open, fully aware of the battle we are in the middle of, and the magnitude of what's at stake. This is the place of action in the Kingdom. Action in the flesh is sweaty, hard work on behalf of others. Action in the Kingdom is a co-laboring with Christ in prayer, and believing for His power to do the heavy lifting.

He calls us to pray with our spiritual eyes wide open, fully aware of the battle we are in the middle of, and the magnitude of what's at stake.

When Tanya and I lived in Seattle, WA, we took frequent trips back home on a connecting flight through Denver. On one of those trips, I was traveling by myself because Tanya had flown back a few days prior. I was waiting for my connection in the Denver airport when I dozed off. I have no problem falling asleep in public.

In this particular case, it almost got the best of me. The gate opened up and they began calling groups of passengers. They boarded everyone except me and were getting ready to close the gate. Thankfully someone had the compassion to nudge me and ask me if I was waiting for this flight. I shot out of my seat because my heart had skipped a beat. I found my boarding pass, and got on the plane. Everything was ok, but it was only because of the mercy of one fellow traveler that I made my flight.

Jesus painted a picture of prayer that seems similar to me waiting for this flight. I knew the plane was taking off; I even knew the scheduled time of departure. The key was remaining alert and not dozing off. The risk in dozing off is the risk of missing out. I wonder how many times we miss out on the action and adventure of the Kingdom because we aren't alert and watchful when we pray. If our eyes are wide open and we are alert in prayer, we understand that things change when we pray.

I hope you understand the simplicity of real, powerful prayer that Jesus describes. It's not about the combination of right words; it's the fervor, passion and urgency in our prayer that reflects our understanding of the power of prayer. Watch and pray.

To close this chapter out, I want to share some practical habits that have helped me move past boredom in prayer to real action.

1. **Walk and pray.** Jesus said watch and pray and you can't walk with your eyes closed. I have found walking or pacing helps me physically engage with the conversation of prayer.

2. **Praying out loud.** I'm not sure where the habit of praying silently came from, but there is no account of silent prayer in the Bible. I have found that opening my mouth and praying out loud helps me resist distractions.

3. **Praying Scripture.** Praying Scripture is the one-two punch of Kingdom action. Praying Scripture demonstrates faith that God's Word truly is a double-edged sword.

Experience It

Confession

Take time to simply "call it like it is" and confess before the Lord that your flesh is real and it is weak. If you're distracted or bored, there's no reason to beat yourself up about it. Confess that "the spirit willing, and the flesh is weak."

Profession

Declare your desire to "watch and pray", to be alert and fully awake to the things on God's heart.

CHAPTER 12

Personal Prayer

Truth #12
Everyone can have a secret place of prayer.

But when you pray, go into your room and
shut the door and pray to your Father who is in secret.
And your Father who sees in secret will reward you.
Matthew 6:6

We have a busy house. With four young kids, the house does not lack volume or energy. But imagine my four kids are downstairs in our house playing away. I call out to them one at a time so I can talk to them individually. I call out for my son and he hears me calling. He shouts back, "In a minute Dad." But he gets distracted and never comes. I wait, and wait, and wait. I call for my oldest daughter, "Luci will you come here for a moment?" She is immersed in playing with her Barbie dolls and doesn't even hear me. I call out for my second daughter, and she giggles but is having fun and keeps playing. Finally, I call out to my youngest. Not only does she hear me, she comes running up the stairs. I pick her up and we go off to have a quality father/daughter moment.

In that scenario, my youngest was rewarded with something the others missed out on: quality time with her father. Something similar was available to each of my kids, but it was only my youngest that received the reward. My love for my other kids doesn't change one bit. I love them no matter what, but there's no arguing that they missed out on a moment with their father.

In this final chapter, I want to help you hear and respond to the Father's call in your life to meet with Him in the secret place. As discussed in the first chapter, God has created you for a relationship with Him. Much of that relationship is grown and developed in day-to-day life. But part of that relationship has to be formed in the secret place of alone-time with God. Nothing can replace that.

As a pastor, I have grown concerned lately with how our society has become overly saturated with media, entertainment, busyness and materialism. We have accumulated so much stuff that the complexity of our lives seems to grow exponentially. We get a new house with a bigger lawn, but it just takes more time to mow that lawn. Within that cultural dynamic, I have seen a decline in spiritual hunger and intimacy with Jesus. The accumulation of things does something to deaden our souls. We begin to grow numb to the presence of Jesus as we are overwhelmed by all of our worldly obligations. We are so easily distracted and often answer the call of the Father with, "In a minute Dad." I so desire to see this change in our lifetimes. I want to see our church become a community of people that are tangibly in love with Jesus. I long to see us step into a season of urgency, passion and vision for intimacy with Jesus.

In the verse that opens this chapter, Jesus is teaching on prayer in its purest form. He is countering the hypocritical prayer of the day, which was done for show and affirmation of others. Prayer with that motivation receives its reward immediately. People are impressed, but that's the extent of the reward.

However, prayer at its best is prayer in the secret place—just you and the Father. No pretenses, no performance, no distractions, no false motives, just you and your heavenly Father.

This is available to every single person in our church. This verse alone is proof of the call of God on your life for personal daily relationship with your Creator. He invites you into a moment with Him saying, "Go into your room and shut the door and talk with Me." The reward is there waiting for you. God's rewards for us cannot be compared to what anyone else receives. Comparison in the Kingdom is never helpful. When we get alone with God and pray from our hearts, we receive a reward that we simply would not receive otherwise.

It's hard for me to describe how pivotal this truth has been in my life. I had a complex time in childhood where I thought that no one wanted to hang out with me. I remember early in elementary school inviting a couple friends to my birthday party, but they turned me down. For some reason, that stuck with me and convinced me that no one wanted to be my friend. It stuck with me for years. I continued on through elementary and middle school being extremely shy and introverted. One day in middle school, my father had a conversation with me that I will never forget. We were talking about transferring me to a different school. I really wanted to transfer, because that was the school Tanya went to, and I thought she was the most beautiful girl in the world. That day, my father made me promise him I would make friends. He said, "Drew, if you go to this school, you need to promise me you will make friends." I responded with a sincere promise to make friends.

> *The God of the Universe wants to spend time with you. He loves you and He likes you.*

I wasn't shy because I disliked people. I loved people. I was shy because for some reason, I believed the lie that no one wanted to hang out with me. I wonder if sometimes we have a hard time believing that God wants to spend time with us? The God of the Universe wants to spend time with each one of us. He loves you and He *likes* you. Get in the secret place and discover that.

Around the time when I started making friends in my new school, I also encountered something that really catalyzed my personal relationship with God. It was at a youth retreat and I responded to a call to receive the baptism in the Holy Spirit. I responded whole-heartedly and truly desired all that God had for me. Then and there, I encountered the person of the Holy Spirit in way that has since transformed my personal time with God. That day I received a prayer language. A prayer language is intimate between God and I, and helps me pray in a way that supersedes what I can articulate in my own words. It truly has transformed my time alone with Jesus.

A personal prayer language is rooted firmly in Scripture: from the three accounts of the baptism of the Holy Spirit explicitly accompanied by tongues (Acts 2, 10, and 19), to the Apostle Paul distinguishing between praying with our minds and praying with the spirit. He said, "For if I pray in tongues, my spirit is praying, but I don't understand what I am saying" (1 Corinthians 14:14 NLT). He goes on to say, "I will *pray in the spirit*, and I will pray in words I understand. I will *sing in the spirit* and I will also sing in words I understand" (1 Corinthians 14:15 NLT, emphasis added).

Paul went on to say, "I thank God that I speak in tongues more than any of you. But in a church meeting I would rather speak five understandable words to help others than ten thousand words in an unknown language" (1 Corinthians 14:18-19 NLT). Paul was emphasizing the best and most essential place for praying in the spirit (or tongues). It was alone, in secret with God. Paul said he prayed more in the spirit alone than any of them. I'm confident that's why Paul emphasizes that type of personal and powerful prayer as he talking about equipping every believer for daily battle in Ephesians 6. He says we should be, "praying in the spirit at all times."

Sadly, I believe sometimes tongues spoken publicly in our worship gatherings have distracted individuals from the personal power of a prayer language in private. Some hear a person pray in tongues in a worship or prayer gathering and think, 'I will never pray in tongues publicly; therefore, praying in tongues isn't for me.' That breaks my heart because it reverses the order of priority from what we just read in Scripture. We read that praying in tongues is, first and foremost, for personal edification; therefore, it is essentially private. So, our thinking should be, 'God equip me with everything I need personally to grow in daily relationship with You, and publicly, I submit to however You want to use me to build up others (which may or may not ever include a public tongue).'

I am so passionate about every individual in our church getting alone with God—finding a place where they can cry out to God and hear from God like never before. I am passionate about seeing a church full of people, in different seasons and from different backgrounds, but all falling more in love with Jesus.

God, awaken Your church with the truth of Your Word. I pray we would take seriously what is before us. You have given us one life to live and called us to things that are bigger than ourselves. We desperately need you! We need you TODAY. Move in our midst and grip our hearts through prayer. Awaken Your church to be the praying church You have called her to be. We love you Jesus!

If you are looking for a little more practical help on personal time with God then check out the appendix called "Making Time to Be Alone with God."

If you want to learn more about your prayer language, I wrote an appendix called "Receiving the Baptism in the Holy Spirit."

Experience It

Confession

Take time to confess any performance or religious pride that has stolen the reward of prayer.

Profession

Declare a fresh desire to get alone with God and develop a secret place of prayer.

Making Time to Be Alone with God

I wanted to make sure to give some instruction for those just starting off in a personal relationship with Jesus. This section will give some straightforward, practical thoughts to help you grow with God as you give Him time.

1. Make a decision ahead of time.

Many times, good intentions don't result in anything substantial. It's not until I make a decision and a plan to actually do something that I find myself following through. Several years ago, I came across an idea in a book titled *Who You Are When No One Is Looking* by Bill Hybels. He talks about the idea of advanced decision-making, which refers to setting things in motion or preparation so that when the time comes it's as though the decision has already been made.

He gives the example of waking up early. If you have the intention of waking up earlier in the morning, then make decisions or preparations the night before so as to make the decision easier when morning actually comes. Maybe that means setting your clothes out the night before. Maybe that means setting your alarm clock across the room so you have to get out of bed. Maybe it means setting the coffee maker on a timer so the coffee is going before you wake up.

When it comes to time with God, I have found that it happens much more often when I decide in advance and prepare for my time with God.

2. Find a place.

Jesus went to "desolate places" or locations where he could truly be alone. It's hard to find a desolate place in our day because of the quantity of noise and distractions. I encourage you to be intentional about finding a place where you can turn off your phone and where you feel freshly inspired to simply be with God.

I have had seasons in my life where I literally met with God in a closet. I spent a year with a desk in a walk-in closet because I was determined to have a place of few distractions. I have had seasons of meeting with God down by a lake near our house. The calm water early in the morning was helpful for me in slowing down to seek Jesus. I have continued to find different places in different seasons so as to maintain an aloneness with God.

3. Have a plan for your prayer time.

I hesitate to give too much direction in developing a rhythm for your prayer time because there is no secret formula for an awesome prayer time. So, instead I'll give you a number of examples and then encourage you to develop a plan that works for you.

The Lord's Prayer

When Jesus was asked by His disciples how to pray, He answered with what has become known as the Lord's Prayer. Jesus did not intend for this prayer to be repeated verbatim as though it were the only way to pray. But, within it, Jesus gave us a beautiful example of the important elements in personal prayer.

Our Father in Heaven, Hallowed be Your Name. Jesus started by setting His Father apart from all else. He starts by declaring praise of Who His heavenly Father is. This is a great way to start prayer, simply by praising God and lifting Him above all else with your words.

Your Kingdom come, Your will be done, on earth as it is in heaven. Jesus then gives an example of praying God's will upon situations, people, places or lives. This prayer for God's will is not just a prayer of trust in God's sovereignty. It is also a bold prayer for God's will as revealed through His Kingdom to be brought about on earth, just like it is in heaven. This is a prayer that can change the demeanor of your prayer life because Jesus is equipping us to pray for His Kingdom to come and will to be done in our families, in our workplaces, in our bodies, in relationships and so on. We can humbly pray for knowledge of God's will for us and the power to carry it out, since God knows what's best for us.

Give us this day our daily bread. God is our source. It is good to acknowledge that on a regular basis. The Father sees what we need, and He alone is our provider. He will give us everything we need if we just ask Him.

And forgive us our debts as we also have forgiven our debtors. Forgiveness is two parts. It's freely receiving forgiveness from our Savior and it's then freely giving forgiveness to those who wrong us. Prayer is the place where true forgiveness starts.

And lead us not into temptation, but deliver us from the evil one. Prayer is conversation about daily living. That means victory for today, freedom for today, release from temptations for today, declarations about the truth for today. This type of prayer equips us to do battle in this life and see God as our deliverer.

Prayer Cards
For the last few years, I've been creating prayer cards to guide my prayer time. Each prayer card has three or four Scripture passages on it and a different topic or area of focus.

For example, I have a prayer card for intimacy with God, my identity in God, my marriage, my wife and each of my kids. These cards have helped me be consistent and persistent in praying over the most important areas of my life by incorporating Scripture into these prayers.

Journaling
Writing prayers out in a journal can be a very practical way of not allowing your wandering mind to steal

the day. In my experience, prayers that I write out are more raw and honest and also become an amazing chronicle of my walk with Jesus.

4. Have a plan for time in the Word.

The last area I want to highlight is being proactive with seeking God through His Word. We are so blessed to live in these times. We have more Bibles at our fingertips than in any time in history, but that doesn't mean we are actually consuming more of the Word. I propose making a plan for taking in more quality time in the Word on a daily basis.

In my journey with God, I have taken many different approaches to consuming God's Word. Here are a few things that have worked for me.

Bible reading plan

There are lots of Bible reading plans that give you a simple, clear direction of passages to read. The nice thing about Bible reading plans is they come in all shapes and sizes. There are dozens of Bible reading plans available on the YouVersion Bible app.

One reading plan we did for a year as a church is the ReadScripture Bible reading plan. It's available on the ReadScripture app and every book is accompanied by a short video explaining how the book fits into the overarching redemptive story of Jesus. It is a powerful way to go through the Bible in one year.

Focus on a book of the Bible

I have found in different seasons that slowing down and consuming one book of the Bible over a longer period of time is extremely helpful in my relationship with Jesus. I have actually taken the time to write a personal, verse-by-verse commentary on Romans, Galatians and Isaiah. These exercises helped me consume the Word on a much deeper level.

Focus on a character or theme of the Bible

There are seasons when God is highlighting certain figures or truths in the Bible for me. I believe it is wise to slow down and take considerable time to study those ideas. It may be studying the life of Moses and journaling through it. It may be studying grace. There are so many possibilities of themes or biblical characters that God wants to speak to you about through His Word.

Mark it up

I encourage everyone to study the Word by making notes, highlighting, underlining, etc. I believe this is helpful because it helps us slow down and think about the words we are reading. As you read the Bible over a lifetime, you will see that different words or themes stick out to you and minister to your life in different ways at different times.

Closing

The key to alone-time with God is that you truly are getting *quality* alone-time with Him. It's not about the quantity of time, checking off an item on your to-do list or accomplishing a chore. It truly is about authentic connection to grow your relationship with God. If you are ever struggling to spend time with God, think of Genesis 3:8 where it says that God walked in the garden in the cool of the morning. Imagine yourself walking with God in a garden. How would you talk with Him? This relationship is what you are created for.

Receiving the Baptism in the Holy Spirit

I n chapter 12, I discussed the gift of a personal prayer language, which is available to all believers for personal encouragement. I want to give some additional biblical instructions on what this is, and how you can receive this gift.

Very simply, baptism in the Holy Spirit is when we experience an encounter with, or immersion in, the Holy Spirit, which is separate from, and only comes after, salvation. This is the promise that Jesus talked about in Luke 24:48, Acts 1:4-5 and Acts 1:8. At this point, the resurrected Christ had already appeared to the disciples, breathed on them, and said, "Receive the Holy Spirit" (see John 20: 22). Now He is telling them to wait in Jerusalem for this "promise of the

Father", which is a reference to a prophecy in Joel Chapter 2 which says "In these last days, I will pour out My Spirit on all flesh..."

This promise of the Father, or baptism in the Holy Spirit, as Jesus calls it, never has constraints on who would receive it. It is a promise for all who believe.

A common misconception about the baptism in the Holy Spirit is that it implies some sort of higher level of spirituality. As I said in prior chapters in this book, comparison in the Kingdom is never helpful. Instead, I encourage people to humbly read the Scriptures and then eagerly seek God for all that He promises us. It is not about what others have or don't have in God, but what the Word of God makes available to each of us personally that should determine what we pursue.

Here are some thoughts that might be helpful as you seek to receive the baptism in the Holy Spirit.

1. Baptism in the Holy Spirit is for you.

When Peter talks about the Holy Spirit being poured out on 120 believers in the second chapter of Acts, he points the people to Joel Chapter 2. Joel's prophecy couldn't make it any clearer that this is for each one of us. He says, "the Holy Spirit will be poured out on *all flesh* (emphasis added)", both young and old, sons and daughters, even the male and female servants (Acts 2:16-18). He emphasizes the breadth of the outpouring of the Holy Spirit to include all generations, all socioeconomic backgrounds, and both men and women alike.

To add to that, Luke goes on to emphasize the outpouring of the Holy Spirit across cultural divides. He gives an example of Jewish (Acts 2) and Samaritan believers (Acts 8) receiving. The Samaritans had Jewish heritage, but over the centuries they had intermarried with other cultures, so they were distinctly different from the Jewish people. And finally, Luke emphasizes the outpouring of the Holy Spirit on Gentiles, which is the rest of us (Acts 10). It's important to catch that Luke is explaining how the promise of the Father is for all people.

2. The purpose of the baptism in the Holy Spirit.

It's important to understand the purpose of the baptism in the Holy Spirit as we pursue what we read about in Scripture. We see that, first and foremost,

God pours out this gift of the Holy Spirit to empower us to be on His mission. He says, "You will receive power when the Holy Spirit has come upon you, and you will be My witnesses in Jerusalem, Judea, Samaria, and to the ends of the earth" (Acts 1:8).

We see a precedent in Scripture that can set our expectation. We see individuals speaking in other tongues after they receive this infilling of the Holy Spirit in Acts 2, 10 and 19. It is also implied in the account of Saul receiving the baptism in the Holy Spirit (Acts 9) because we know that he prays in tongues from 1 Corinthians 14. Even though this is the expectation, I believe it's important to keep in mind the purpose set forth by Jesus. We can expect a prayer language, but for what end?

The purpose is for you and I to live, filled and equipped, to represent Jesus in this world. Our need for this type of equipping is seen so clearly in Peter's life. Before the baptism in the Holy Spirit, he lied to a little girl about whether he knew Jesus (Matthew 26:69). After he was baptized in the Holy Spirit, he was compelled to share the good news of Jesus with thousands (Acts 2).

The purpose isn't just to receive a prayer language. It is so much more. An intimate prayer language is just one way God equips us to live life to the fullest.

3. Know the heart of the Father.

As you begin to seek this filling or baptism in the Holy Spirit, remind yourself about the heart of the Father. This is the promise of your heavenly Father and He doesn't play tricks on us.

Jesus reminds us of this by saying, "For everyone who asks receives, and the one who seeks finds, and to the one who knocks it will be opened. What father among you, if his son asks for a fish, will instead of a fish give him a serpent; or if he asks for an egg, will give him a scorpion? If you then, who are evil, know how to give good gifts to your children, how much more will the heavenly Father give the Holy Spirit to those who ask him!" (Luke 11:10-13)

Not only does He know what we need, but He delights in giving us those good gifts for His purposes. As you seek God for this promise, remind yourself of the character of your heavenly Father. He can be trusted.

4. It is for lifestyle change, not just a one-time experience.

If we truly believe the baptism in the Holy Spirit is for the purpose of empowering us to represent Him, then we would expect to be filled with power time and time again as we walk in relationship with Him. Sometimes the baptism in the Holy Spirit gets reduced to a one-time experience. When that happens, we miss the purpose it was intended for.

The church in Acts understood this. They had received an outpouring of the Holy Spirit earlier, and they had seen thousands come to know Christ. In fact, people were coming to know Christ daily. But soon, persecution rose up against the church, and the church recognized their need. They knew they needed fresh boldness and power to continue moving on in God's mission. They cried out to God and prayed, "'And now, Lord, look upon their threats and grant to Your servants to continue to speak Your word with all boldness, while You stretch out Your hand to heal, and signs and wonders are performed through the Name of Your holy servant Jesus.' And when they had prayed, the place in which they were gathered together was shaken, and they were all filled with the Holy Spirit and continued to speak the word of God with boldness" (Acts 4:29-31).

I encourage each of us to believe God for exactly what we need for today. Many days, that means I ask God to be filled again with fresh boldness and confidence, not to play it safe, and to represent Him well. As I pray that way, often I then feel compelled to pray in my prayer language, and it's when I am edified by the Holy Spirit that I am equipped and built up, and I can walk into the world with vision and willingness to do whatever it takes to fulfill God's will in my life.

Closing

I encourage you to simply take God at His Word. If you ask God for promises you see in Scripture that are clearly for all people, God honors those prayers. Get alone with God or ask a friend or leader in your life to lay their hands on you and pray that you would be filled with the Holy Spirit.

Acknowledgments

It is such an honor to follow Jesus alongside such a courageous group of people. I want to take a moment to show gratitude to a number of people who were instrumental in this project. First of all, my wife is my life-long prayer companion and biggest encouragement. Tanya, I am so grateful to God for you. I also want to thank Kyle Trosen, Tony Meyer, Kayla Meyer and Dean Meyer for their comments and contributions. I need to thank the LifePointe staff for their prayer and encouragement throughout: Nicole Gilson, Joe & Paige McGovern, and Riley & Shena Edwards. And finally, I have to acknowledge and extend tremendous gratitude to Laura Saunders for her excellent editorial skills. Her countless hours and constant back and forth really made this project the best it could be.

About the Author

Drew Meyer is the lead pastor at LifePointe Church in Ames, IA. Drew and his family moved to Ames in 2011 to start a campus ministry to Iowa State University. His love for Ames and the local expression of the church through LifePointe has only grown. His desire is to see the church live out and experience the life-giving power of the message of Jesus. For more information go to: www.livethemessage.org.

Made in the USA
San Bernardino, CA
17 December 2018